A PATHWAY TO FREEDOM
An Introduction to
Centering Prayer Workbook

Dr. Savario Mungo   *Marietta Della Penna*

DEDICATION

This workbook is dedicated to those men and women who wish their darkness will be pierced by Light, whose pain will be transformed into Joy, and whose hope someday will be deepened by love.

IN REMEMBRANCE

FRED ECKART

Fred was an inspiration to many of us who
were involved in Prison Ministry. He was the
Contemplative Outreach Ltd. Faculty member
in charge of the organizations prison ministry
outreach. In this capacity, Fred offered advice,
materials and encouragement to those of us willing
to work in prison settings. His experience and
compassion will be sorely missed.

ACKNOWLEDGEMENTS

We wish to thank Contemplative Outreach Ltd. for providing the training and resources for the co-authors to become certified presenters, and thus knowledgeable in the method of centering prayer and its dissemination. This training, combined with resources available through CO and an interest and experience in prison ministry, has led to the development of this workbook.

For the opportunity to go into the prison settings in the Texas system and introduce the inmates to the method of Centering prayer we would like to thank Chaplain Robert Kibbee of the McConnell Unit, who gave the first extended opportunity to work with the men in a variety of spiritual activities, including centering prayer, and Chaplain Robert Styers of the Garza East Unit, who allowed the teaching of classes in his facility. Without their help and support, the experience needed to develop a program for teaching this prayer in correctional facilities would not have been possible. In addition, their support made it possible to have the inmates share the editing of this final document.

This material was field tested over a year and a half at two different prisons. The final stage in completing this book was to submit the chapters to inmates in the prisons who had completed the introduction to Centering Prayer, and were willing to help in the editing of the final manuscript. Their assistance allowed us to develop materials that were "inmate friendly," and would be more easily used by a variety of inmates. The following men, from four different institutions in the Texas system, each voluntarily read and edited multiple chapters of the workbook. The names are listed here with their consent.

Clark Norris	Joseph Walker	Carlos Elizondo
Henry Dominquez	Linroy Davis	Harold Orndorff
Larry Gallien	Tom Seils	Elias Flores
Michael Harris	Izzy Reynaldo	Lorenzo Esquivel
Frank Ortiz	Jose Valera	Dennis Chandler

MY CENTERING PRAYER

There's more to me than there used to be
'Cause of a new highway I've been shown.
Actually it's a simple narrow path
And I walk it all alone.

I'm asked to go inside my mind
And work through the turmoil there.
Go past my thoughts, emotions and dreams
Forget my sins and all my cares.

The secret it seems is to slow my mind
And that's not easily done.
But I push thoughts away with my Sacred Word
And remove them one by one.

As each thought leaves, I travel deeper
Into a more uncluttered mind.
I catch a glimpse of the solitary place
I have such needs to find.

I find the pool of solitude.
I've been here times before.
But now I have needs to travel further
Than to just sit here on the shore.

I feel this unexplainable urge
To answer to the calling.
To slide beneath the surface
And all at once; I'm falling.

I push the thoughts of fear away
Using my sacred word.
And I find myself in a silent world
The likes I've never heard.

I've slipped into the fringes of my soul
And have a glimpse of eternal things
One more step in the same direction
And I could hear Angels sing?

But the idea here is to be available to God
And to show Him you'll make the trip.
None of us are perfect
We'll make mistakes; everyone will slip.

When the bell rings, it's back to reality
And you'll not really know where you've been.
But you'll have this very satisfied feeling
You've reserved some time for Him.

Joe Walker- TDCJ

ABOUT THE AUTHORS

Savario Mungo

Dr. Mungo has over 40 years experience in teaching at levels from elementary to college. In addition he has spent over 20 years in prison ministry in four states. He has been involved with Centering Prayer for over 14 years, has been a chapter coordinator for CO chapters in two communities in Texas and is a Contemplative Outreach Ltd. commissioned presenter.

Marietta Della Penna

Marietta is a retired teacher of English with a Masters degree in Theology. She has been involved in the Centering Prayer movement for 15 years. She has taught deacons for the Syracuse diocese, and has served as as Spiritual Director and Director of Retreats at her local parish.

OVERVIEW OF THIS WORKBOOK

The main purpose of this workbook is to help you discover your life in the Spirit by embarking on an inner journey.

To begin this journey, as in any journey, we need things that help make the journey easier and more comfortable. We also need to let go of baggage that would weigh us down and deprive us of the pleasure of the journey.

Among the things that will make the journey easier are the practices of centering prayer and Lectio Divina. This book will teach you these practices.

The workbook is divided into 12 chapters.
Chapter 1 will address God in our Lives, and the view of God as we grew up.
Chapter 2 will deal with what is most basic in our lives – our relationship with God. This chapter will lead us through the various types of prayers and will open the way for an understanding of Centering Prayer.

A detailed study of the Method of Centering Prayer will be given in Chapters 3 and 4.
Chapter 5 will address a most important part of Centering Prayer – Thoughts & The Sacred Word. This chapter will provide answers to many of the questions you may have regarding this practice, and will help you to understand the more subtle points of the practice.

In chapter 6 a traditional way of reading Scripture, known as Lectio Divina, will be introduced. Both of these practices (which are at the heart of this workbook) will be reviewed again and again.

Chapters 7&8 will focus on our relationship with God, and the fruits of the Holy Spirit that are given to us through the practice of Centering Prayer and Lectio Divina.
Both of these chapters will open us up to the results we'll see in ourselves, in others, and in daily life as a result of these practices.

In chapters 9, 10 & 11 you'll be given three more practices:
The Active Prayer
The Welcoming Prayer
The Prayer of Forgiveness
These prayers are given so that the presence of God may be more easily accessed in our daily lives.
Chapter 12 is a final review and summary

We pray that your journey may be rich and full of light

Savario Mungo
Marietta Della Penna

Smungo1959@aol.com
febpac@yahoo.com

TABLE OF CONTENTS

CHAPTER 1

<u>GOD IN OUR LIVES</u>

"We love God because God first loved us." (John 1 4:19)

This is a pretty powerful quote, so how do we respond to it? Do we get it?

We've heard it before - from parents, church, or in Sunday school, but do we believe it?

If we don't, here may be some reasons why:

To believe this statement we have to trust God. But too often our childhood education, religious instruction, parents, environment, may have made trust difficult. This is because the model we were taught- often called the "Western Model," contained some of the following ideas:

WESTERN MODEL

- God is out there someplace, apart from us- He is not with us, he is "somewhere else" apart from us.

- External(outside) acts(deeds) are more important than internal acts(acts from within) - what you do as seen by others is most important – the "Holy Joe" image. We do things to "look" Christian, or what we think people like to see as "Christian" with little real conviction.

- We do good things so God can reward us and then go to Heaven. God judges us every day. We believe in a "Getcha Gotcha" God. We must please him or we will not go to heaven.

- Strong belief is on future rewards and happiness. What we want is a good life in Heaven, not realizing we get rewards in the here and now as well.

In addition, we may believe that he's angry with us or isn't concerned about what happens to us. We've never seen him face to face. When we die we'll simply be dead. End of story.

Besides, who can answer these questions:

Where was God on 9/11?
Where was God in Viet Nam, in Iraq, in Africa?
Where's God when children are dying of aids?

Where's God when he knows I'm innocent and I end up in here?
Where was God when I was growing up and being abused?
Where was God when I had to hang out on streets and steal in order to survive?

The answer is simple: He's been there all the time.
Oh yeah? Prove it!

The Bible tells us that we're made in the image and likeness of God. Right from the start God placed his image on our souls. After all, when we love someone don't we want to become like him or her? Or take them and make them part of ourselves? So it is with God. He loved us so much that he became one of us. Jesus didn't come to earth only to save us. He came because God wanted to experience what it's like to be a human being. And God continues to experience what that's like through us.

When we want to know more about ourselves we're said to be on a "spiritual journey." It's difficult to get off to a good start on this journey if we're carrying around a negative attitude about God, or some of the ideas contained in the "Western Model" of religious understanding. The following "Scriptural Model" might help.

SCRIPTURAL MODEL (based on the Bible)

Our interior motivation(inner drive) is more important than external acts(outside deeds).

God wants to know where your heart's at. If your heart is in the right place, external acts will come naturally.

God is within each of us as well as being "out there."

God lives within us, we cannot change that fact. When we journey within ourselves, we will meet God.

Strong belief is on the effort to love God here and now and to serve others, not on rewards we might receive in Heaven

To reap the benefits of someone's love, we must love them in return. Live for today and love God today.

God loves us no matter what we do. He does not judge us every day. We cannot "earn" God's love.

God loves us. The peace comes from loving Him in return. He's not here to pass judgment on you. He wants your love.

GOD IN OUR LIVES

A faithful Christian is one who lives the Gospel, not only reads it or tries, in the reading, to manipulate God to fit our current problems.

Treat God with respect. He wants you to live in his world and be honest and "straight up" with Him.

 The spiritual journey is really a "journey within." Going deep inside ourselves to learn who we really are, what makes us tick, our feelings, fears and driving forces is hard work. Usually it's scary because we aren't sure of what we'll find, or know what we will find and are afraid God will not love us as we are! And we're not sure what to do with what we find!

For this reason many of us don't even try. What if I find that I'm a responsible person who can succeed in life in whatever I try? How much work or change is it going to take to pull it off? Or what if I'm really a "clutz"- not very swift in mind or body? H   arted? It's very easy to just give up, lick my "wound   something else. Why do we do this? Probably be   soon becomes clear to us that we may also be confi   s fear or shame that sounds like this:

"Because of   doesn't want to bother with me until I clean up my   ?"

If we believe   t God doesn't want to have anything to do with us,   mpletely wrong.

We have a co   ne - not the world, not what we've done, nor ever   ver take away. It remains a part of us in the afterlife   eve or not.

Our job on ear   ss in ourselves by believing that we are good, and b

Remember that   hteous, but for sinners and for the poor. We can be   poor in background, education, by being shut out   ng empty inside, - and by feeling despair over any   our life.

Jesus knows tha   ponsible for our actions, there's so much that co   d - family, an abusive childhood, fear, having to su   ot believing in ourselves, feeling unworthy, and, m   as basically good.

Jesus does not ju   en he looks at us, all he sees is this core of goodn   over his shoulders like so much garbage.

The trouble with us is that we can't accept love, let alone accept unconditional love. It's too much for us. We don't know what to do with it. It overwhelms us, even making us fearful because we think something is being demanded of us. But that's the point. Love that is unconditional never demands anything from us. Unconditional love simply loves.

Like Jesus, when the Father looks at us, he sees only the good regardless of how hidden and buried it is within us. We don't see it and don't want to see it. But the Father sees nothing else.

Remember in John's Gospel when Jesus prays to his Father, he says:

" Father, may they be one in us,
as you are in me and I am in you,
so that the world may believe it was you who sent me.
I have given them the glory you gave me,
that they may be one as we are one.
With me in them and you in me,
may they be so completely one
that the world will realize that it was you who sent me
And that I have loved them as much as you have loved me." (John17 21:23)

" I pray that the love with which you loved me may be in them,
so that I may be in them." (John 17 :26)

Jesus isn't praying for creatures from outer space! He's praying for us!

We are **never separate** from God. We only **think** we are. He is the foundation of our existence as well as the love that moves the moon and the stars. How much more then does this love desire us who, unlike the moon and the stars, are created in his image?

All he asks is for us to believe. And if, for whatever reason, we can't as yet believe, we can **pretend to believe and then see what happens!**

Long ago a wise man from the East wrote these words:

"I concerned myself to remember God, to know him, to love him, to seek him. When I had come to the end of my life, I saw that he had remembered me long before I had remembered him; that his knowledge of me had preceded my knowledge of him; that his love toward me had existed before my love of him, and that he had sought me before I had sought him."

AN ENCOUNTER WITH JESUS

(guided meditation)

Close your eyes, sit in a comfortable position, and relax.

With each breath breathe in the Holy Spirit and exhale light and peace to the world.

Do this for a few minutes, and then relax.

Now, imagine you're sitting on a rocky mountain. The day is warm, yet there's a cool breeze blowing. In the distance you can see snow-capped mountains, and down below there are hills of wildflowers – yellow, white, blue, and pink wildflowers. They seem to be bowing to the sun as the wind passes over them. You look immediately below you at the hard surface of a large rock. Suddenly, a shadow passes over it. You become startled, perhaps a bit frightened, and you quickly turn around ready to defend yourself against what it could be.

You're ready for a fight if need be, but when you turn you see an unarmed man, defenseless, with the trace of a smile upon his lips.

"A magnificent view, isn't it?" he says.

There's something about this guy you don't get, something strange, yet …

"Yeah," you answer.

"I remember years ago when I knelt on rocks like these, only they were in a garden."

"Were you planting something?" You didn't know how to respond to this guy.

"No, as a matter of fact I was praying. It was a desperate time for me."

You don't know what to say next, but heck you might as well try.

"What were you praying for?"

"For something to be taken away from me, yet knowing all the time I had to go through with it," he responded.

"Oh, seems like I've heard something like this before – way back when I was a kid, but I'll be damned if I can remember it."

"Perhaps you read it, or heard it in a church?"

"Church? Are you kiddin'? And I don't read all that much either!"

And then something in you begins to stir – an image, a word, a memory – long ago – a man –miracles – preaching – loving – suffering – and…

"Nah, what am I thinking of anyway - I'm imagining - have to be – am I nuts? He certainly wouldn't speak to someone like me – get a grip on yourself…

And yet, he sat with people like me, talked with them, cured them…and loved them."

Then he turns to you and says:

"Why is it so hard to trust what you see and what you're thinking?"

"I don't know," you reply, "it's just that you may be God, for God's sake, and God doesn't come around talking to the likes of me, or anyone else for that matter."

"Oh, but he does. All the time. And yet he's not seen nor recognized. My poor people have such low images of themselves no matter how hard I try to convince them that they were made in the image of my Father and me, and are loved unconditionally. And because of this poor image, they couldn't possibly trust that I'm in every thought, in every situation no matter how horrible. In fact, it's in the worst situations that I'm most present. All I wish to do is for them to accept my love. That's all. When this happens everything else will fall into place."

"You make it sound so simple."

"It is simple because God is simple."

"Well, what if I accept everything you're saying? Then what?"

"Then, simply relax and be yourself. But speak to me – it's very important – for your sake. Prayer is the most important thing there is. How else can I communicate directly with you and you with me? How else can you hear me? Even if something comes to you as a result of another person or as a result of reading something, it's because you can listen because you've first listened in prayer. Do you understand what I'm saying to you?"

"Yes, I think so."

"Then, please, tell me how you feel."

1- How would you respond to Jesus?
(everything is acceptable – love, anger, fear, hostility and so on)

Assignment:
Before the next class: Read the content for Chapter 2

CHAPTER 2

<u>PRAYER AS RELATIONSHIP</u>

Relationships! Relationships! Relationships! We've all known them, loved them, feared them. But, being human, we can hardly do without them. We have had relationships with friends and family, so we have experienced relationships.

And so it is with God.

Sound silly?   Does God really need a relationship with us? He's God, we say. He's always contained in himself. He doesn't need anyone or anything. Perhaps not. That's one way of looking at it. But the God we know through Jesus wants a relationship with us just as the one he had with Jesus. Sounds impossible, doesn't it? Sounds almost too good to be true. But when we read Jesus' words in the Bible, Jesus is telling us that God loves us unconditionally, and, let's face it, when we, yes, even God, loves someone unconditionally, we want a relationship with them. It can't be otherwise. It's all a part of being human.

And this is where prayer comes in.

What is Prayer?

Prayer is nothing more, nor less, than a loving relationship with God. One type of prayer is **Intercessary Prayer.** This is when we think about prayer, or even pray, and we are asking for something we need, or asking God to turn a situation around, or to influence others, or whatever it might be. But we're asking.   We've done this since we were kids, and will continue to do so.

Then there are **Vocal Prayers**- those prayers we were taught when we were very young, or heard in churches, or were from the Bible, and we usually say these prayers out loud, praising and thanking God. They're prayers created by others and we use their words.

And there is a kind of prayer known as **Reflective Prayer** where we think about something we've read in the Bible, or heard in a sermon, or otherwise, and we pray about it.

Responsive Prayer is when we open ourselves to God in thanksgiving and wonder, and we pray in the moment for the sheer joy of it.

Finally, there's a kind of prayer known as **Contemplative Prayer**. This prayer is a pure gift from God. It doesn't contain any words, or thoughts, or images, or feelings. It's a prayer where we simply rest in God. It's a kind of surrender with our whole being to the presence and mystery of God. This prayer gives us the gift of silence. It puts us on the road to peace, a type of peace only God can give. Long ago, a holy man described this kind of prayer as "the deep knowledge of God steeped in love." This prayer practice is an opportunity to be with God in silence and peace even in the most chaotic environments. In the next section you'll be able to understand more fully what contemplative prayer is really all about, and how it relates to your life in your present environment.

What we must always remember is that our desire, or yearning, even our curiosity about God, is also God's gift to us.

"We love God because God first loved us." (1 John 4:19)

The Christian Contemplative Tradition

In the Christian Tradition, **CONTEMPLATIVE PRAYER** is considered to be the pure gift of God. It is an opening of mind and heart, our whole being to God, the Ultimate Mystery, beyond thoughts, words, and emotions. It is simply resting in the presence of God. To travel in beyond the chaos of our mind and into the silence and peace of God!

The Christian contemplative tradition was summed up by Gregory the Great at the end of the sixth century. He described contemplation as the "deep knowledge of God that is impregnated with love." For Gregory, contemplation was both the fruit of reflecting on the word of God in Scripture and the precious gift of God. He called it "**resting in God.**"

In this "resting" the mind and heart are not so much seeking God as beginning to experience , "to taste", what they have been seeking. This state is not the suspension of all activity, but the reduction of many acts and reflections to a simple movement of consenting to God's presence and action within. We must finally slow down and simply allow God to be! We must give God a chance. He will not kick our door to get to us. He is not that kind of God. We must trust him; even if we've never done so before. From our trust and faith; and our acknowledgement of God being good…comes the peace we all so greatly desire. We must finally give God a chance and accept Him as a loving God!

In Aramaic, the language Jesus spoke, the word for prayer is "shela" (sha-lu). It means "to open oneself", to "listen to" or "to open oneself to the Divine Presence. Prayer was not necessarily saying words or asking for things. "Shela" (sha-lu) is more equivalent to what we call today contemplation.

The Word of God in Scripture and in the example of Jesus Christ is the source of Christian Contemplation. The early writers of the faith frequently explained scriptures from a contemplative perspective. Strengthening one's faith through the gifts of wisdom and understanding, enabled the Christian gradually to perceive. The gifts of the spirit were believed to become fully realized through the regular practice of prayer and the growth of faith into contemplation.

Attitude Toward God

As we begin to look at our prayer life, and move into different ideas about prayer and our relationship with God, it is important to first understand what our attitude is towards God. We develop our attitudes from early childhood, and it could be one filled with fear and rigid views of God or one of trust in a loving God.

The spiritual journey, our movement toward God and our prayer life, has a great difficulty in getting off to a good start if we have various negative attitudes towards God. We need trust in God as a loving God.

Prayer as Relationship

Do you know someone who, shortly after meeting them, you know you do not wish to establish a relationship of any kind with them? Think for a minute of how you communicate with that person.

Do you know someone who is very close to you and who you want to either maintain or increase your relationship with them? Think for a moment of how you communicate with them.

There is a distinct difference in the two ways of communicating referred to above, isn't there? Think about it and how you would communicate differently in these situations.

How we communicate determines the level of our relationship. It's the same with God and prayer- the way we communicate with God.

Steps in a Relationship

Every relationship, if it's true at all, develops through a process of growing intimacy. We move from acquaintanceship to friendliness, to friendship to intimacy. And so does our relationship with Christ. Perhaps the following steps will enable us to see this more clearly.

STEPS IN A RELATIONSHIP

With a Person and   Expressed in Prayer

With Christ

With a Person and With Christ	Expressed in Prayer
Acquaintanceship Informational Formal, awkward	Vocal Prayer Opens us to keep in contact with Christ, ex. grace before meals, going to church or Sunday school. Any contact at all with God begins the acquaintance
Friendliness Conversational Informal/at ease	Reflective Prayer Opens us to allow God to speak to us, impact our Lives, and engage our Faculties and energies. Ex. Experiencing God in nature, Prayerful reading of scripture
Friendship Commitment Self- disclosure Spontaneity/Freedom Confidence/Gratitude Shared joy/suffering	Responsive Prayer Opens our heart, feelings and emotions completely to Christ. Ex. frequent spontaneous prayer. Vocal/silent
Intimacy Self-surrender Experiences Oneness Fidelity to the relationship Being with the other with no need To say, prove or do anything	Contemplative Prayer We begin to experience the peace of God A pure gift opening us to God's presence beyond thoughts, words, and emotions. Ex. Unceasing prayer, aware of God's presence in everyone

Naturally, in this chart, as in all human relationships, there is a certain overlapping that takes place. We go from one to the other and then back again, and that's fine. Centering prayer comes in when we hope to arrive at the final step, that is, contemplative prayer.

Centering prayer is a method that helps us to be prepared to receive the gift of contemplation. But, in addition to being a method, it is also a prayer, a relationship with God that leads us to greater and greater intimacy with him.

On the Gradual Development of Intimacy with God

"The chief thing that separates us from God is the thought that we are separated from him. If we get rid of that thought, our troubles will be greatly reduced. We fail to believe that we are always with God and that he is part

of every reality. The present moment, every object we see, our inmost nature are all rooted in him. But we hesitate to believe this until personal experience gives us confidence to believe in it. This involves the gradual development of intimacy with God. God constantly speaks to us through each others as well as from within. The interior experience of God's presence activates our capacity to perceive him in everything else-in people, in events, in nature."

Open Mind, Open Heart   by Thomas Keating

I urge you to read and reread some of this material. Allow God to work inside of you. There is nothing to fear. We are about to embark upon the removal of obstacles within us that will allow us to have union with God in a deeper way.

Assignment:

Do Daily Activities for Chapter 2

Read content of Chapter 3 for next class

Daily Follow Up Activities

Chapter 2

Day 1

    1. Describe your prayer practice- Include: When do you pray? How often do you pray? What types of prayer do you most often do?

    2. Do you feel more comfortable doing formal or informal prayers?

Explain.

Day 2

Write down the various descriptions of God you remember from your Childhood.

Which of these do you think are still with you today?

Day 3

Read and write down the following Scriptural passages related to Contemplative prayer:

    Psalm 46:10

    Psalm 37:7

    Psalm 62:5

    Hebrews 4:10

    Isaiah 30:15

    Mark 6:30

What characteristics of contemplation can you list from the above scriptural sources?

Day 4

    On Steps in Relationship chart-

PRAYER AS RELATIONSHIP

Give an example of a prayer practice that you would place on each of the first three levels of prayer in the chart.

2.At which level of prayer do you find yourself most often ?

Day 5

Re read the last quote from Thomas Keating.

1. How does any of this quote relate to you and your relationship with God?

CHAPTER 3

METHOD OF CENTERING PRAYER -I

In the last unit we introduced the concept or idea of contemplative prayer and prayer as relationship. Today we will continue with our discussion on prayer to introduce a form of prayer known as **Centering Prayer**

Where does Centering Prayer come from?

First of all, it is a response to the words of Jesus in the Bible:

"…But when you pray, go to your inner room, close the door, and pray to your Father in secret. And your Father who sees in secret will repay you."

(Matthew 6:6)

This is what we do when we enter into Centering Prayer.

We go inside ourselves (the inner room) and we close the door (that is, we leave our thoughts, feelings, emotions, images) and we pray by consenting to the presence and action of God within us.

Centering Prayer was practiced in the Christian tradition for centuries but they didn't call it that, and for the majority of Christians, even contemplative prayer (which centering prayer prepares us for) was not known then and is not known today.

Why?

There are a number of reasons, not the least of which is that it wasn't encouraged because others didn't understand what people were doing, and therefore, was afraid of all sorts of things like the "devil" or evil taking over. At least with vocal prayers everyone knew what he was saying. What others didn't know, but what the saints have known through their experience with contemplative prayer is that this form of prayer is too deep and holy for evil or anything else to creep in. The prayer reaches deep inside us where only God lives. **Nothing can touch this sacred place but God himself.**

Still, contemplative prayer was not encouraged.

However, many saints and mystics and prophets did enter into contemplative prayer because it was in this prayer, that went beyond thoughts and images, where they could experience the living God. And from these men and women we've gained knowledge, especially the knowledge of the love of God for us, upon which rests many answers.

It takes time to develop a deep intimacy with God. But we should never be discouraged.

One Inmates Definition of Centering Prayer:

" Centering prayer allows us the freedom to move past thoughts, feelings, emotions and the images in our minds. The very things that keep us contained within ourselves are the same things that keep us apart from God. Sometimes we feel our mind is continually full of thoughts and feelings we can't seem to control. The emotions that are at war within us and the images that seem tattooed on our minds are just some of the things we will travel past in Centering prayer.

Some of you have already tried to journey past these thoughts, images and emotions through the use of alcohol or drugs, but the final destination always turned out to make things worse.

Centering prayer offers us an opportunity to silence our minds. For once and for all, we have an avenue past ourselves and into the presence of God. You see...the very things we've been talking about (thoughts, feelings, emotions, and images) are the very things that keep us separated from God.

God does not separate Himself form us; we separate ourselves from Him. By gently removing these things from our mind we embark on our journey to the presence of God!

This prayer involves discipline, respect and honesty with yourself, Remember, your journey is to the presence of God and the peace He offers.

How can we turn down the opportunity to find peace in the presence of He who created us?"   (Joseph Walker TDCJ)

He is always inside us waiting to be seen by us. Because we **think** we're apart from him, we make ourselves apart from him. But this is only a thought, certainly not the truth. If we'd throw this thought out the window half our troubles would be over. It takes time to believe that he's firmly placed in us and in everyone around us, yes, even in the people we hate and despise. We can hear him speaking to us through others, or see him in a kind gesture, or in an event that suddenly happens. This takes time but in doing centering prayer, the Holy Spirit, gradually and unknown to us, is working within our very depths, and transforming us so that we can come to see Christ in ourselves, in events in our lives, and in others.

And one day we'll come to realize what Jesus was trying to get across to us with these words:

"When the day comes you will know that I am in my Father and you are in me and I in you." (John 14:20)

The Method of Centering Prayer

We now come to the method of centering prayer. When we learn to do anything new, we need to understand the process, and practice that process. The same is true of Centering Prayer. But what we have to remember is that although we use the word method (which we can apply to so many things), the method of centering prayer is also (since it's a prayer) a relationship with God, and a discipline that is designed to build that relationship.

If you practice this prayer, you can never do it wrong!!

In fact the only way we can do this prayer wrong is **if we don't show**

 up or if we walk out in the middle of the prayer!

The Guidelines

Let's look at the four guidelines:

Choose a sacred word

Sit comfortably with eyes closed and gently introduce the sacred word.

If thoughts are engaged, simply return to the sacred word

At the end of the prayer, remain in silence with eyes closed for a couple of minutes.

The guidelines are easy enough but in order to understand them fully, the following explanations give us a bigger picture.

1-Choose a Sacred Word

A **sacred word** is an expression of our **intention and consent** to God's presence and action in us**. Intention** has been compared to an engagement before marriage; and **consent**, the marriage itself or when we finally say "I do."

Before choosing a sacred word we pray to the Holy Spirit to help us choose one that fits us. It should be a word of one or two syllables. Keep it simple. Some examples are: God, Jesus, Abba, Father, Mother, Mary, Amen, Love, Peace, Mercy, Listen, Silence, Stillness, Faith, Trust, Yes. You may even choose a word from a different language. Be sure the word you pick does not trigger other thoughts associated with the word. For example one person started with the word "Jesus." However every time she said "Jesus", her mind automatically went to the song- "Jesus loves me this I know".…..The person finally settled on a word that did not trigger a song or another thought.

Please understand that there's no such thing as a right or wrong word. What makes the word sacred is not what it means or represents to us, but rather because it's a symbol of our intention and consent to God's presence and action in us.

If we decide to change our sacred word we should not do so while doing the prayer because that would start us thinking again.

2-Sit comfortably with eyes closed and slowly introduce the sacred word

Schedule a moment or time when moving into inner silence is easiest. Take into account the environment around you(T.V., yelling, and other distractions) as you pick a time that is best for you.

Sit comfortably means just that. We can sit on a chair, on the floor, on your bunk, any way that is comfortable. We should try to make ourselves as comfortable as

 possible. It's hard opening up to God while we're in pain, simply because the pain gets our attention and not God. We should try to keep our backs straight with our head up, not hanging down.

We close our eyes in order to let go of everything around us as well as thoughts, images, noises, or memories that may pop into our heads.

Then…gently…we introduce the sacred word to our mind. To remember the "gentle" part is important. We're dealing with the Holy Spirit here and not with our individual wills that often tend to express themselves forcibly.

If we should happen to fall asleep while in prayer, we simply pick it up again upon awakening. We're not to feel guilty or come down hard on ourselves because of it.

A great saint once said something like this:

" A father does not get upset if his child should fall asleep in his arms."

And that's how it is with us as far as God is concerned.

Yet, we should try to be responsive and alert at all times.

3- If thoughts are engaged, simply return to the sacred word

The word "thoughts" in centering prayer is a catch-all word for practically everything. These include:

Body sensations, feelings, images, noises, memories, experiences of the past, plans for the future, reflections, concepts, commentaries and particular spiritual experiences. In other words, EVERYTHING!

In this prayer our goal is to connect to the living God, so everything that is not

God is to be let go.

The only activity we make in this prayer is to return to the sacred word. So, whenever we find ourselves "thinking about a thought" we return ever so gently to the sacred word.

Sometimes we may experience some physical symptoms like itches or twitches, or a slight pain. These are due to the untying of physical knots in the body. What do we do? We return ever so gently to the sacred word.

Sometimes we may notice a heaviness or lightness in our hands or feet. These may be due to a deep level of spiritual awareness. What do we do? We return ever so gently to the sacred word.

Any other activity we may do requires effort and effort refers to the future. When we're in the future, it's impossible to be in the present where God is.

Sometimes the sacred word may become unclear or disappear during the time of centering prayer. As you advance this may happen more and more. Don't worry about it; all it means is that the sacred word has gone inward, that is, more and more inside of us.

An important meaning of the term "**Discipline of Centering Prayer**," refers to your discipline in returning to the sacred word every time you find yourself caught up in thoughts, images, etc. Returning to this sacred word is the key to practicing this prayer.

4. At the End of the prayer period, remain in silence with eyes closed for a couple of minutes.

Those additional minutes help us to bring the atmosphere of silence into daily life.

Even if there's much going on around you, you're able to be quiet and peaceful within.

If the prayer is done with a group, someone should be chosen to recite a prayer (whether it be the Lord's Prayer or another) slowly and gently while the others listen.

At the end of the session, do not try to "score" yourself; or say, "I didn't feel anything." You are not expected to come away with some major revelation. By doing this prayer, you have shown your intention to be in the presence of God. What else happens is not in our control This is a prayer of intention. God wants us to be open to his presence and action within. This session you have done just that. There are no other expectations.

The minimum recommended time for centering prayer is 20 minutes. Two periods are recommended each day, one first thing in the morning, and the other in the afternoon or early evening.

Although 20 minutes is recommended, sometimes finding more time available. The main point is to do the prayer, no matter how much time you may be limited to. There is no limit to your time spent with God.

Definitions:

Contemplative Prayer
A knowledge of God through the intimacy of experiencing his holy presence.

Centering Prayer
A prayer discipline that allows us to be more open to contemplative prayer

*-Centering Prayer is not meant to replace other kinds of prayer, rather it shows a new light and depth of meaning on all types of prayer.

*- Centering Prayer is at the same time a relationship with God and a discipline to support that relationship. It is a movement beyond conversation with Christ to communion with him and prepares us for the gift of contemplation.

A final word about the **sacred word** written by Fr. Thomas Keating:

"The Sacred Word is a way of renewing your intention to open yourself to God and to accept Him as He is. While this does not prevent anyone from praying in other forms at other times, the period of centering prayer is not the time to pray specifically for others. By opening yourself to God, you are implicitly praying for everyone past, present, and future. You are embracing the whole of creation. You are accepting all reality beginning with God and with that part of your own reality of which you may not be generally aware, namely, the spiritual level of your being."

Imagine praying for everyone past, present, and future by simply opening yourself to God. You'll do more good for the world with this prayer than if you were fighting battles, and you will help God just as much. For, whether we believe it or not, we truly are needed." Fr. Thomas Keating in **Open Mind, Open Hear**t: page 43

Close class with a 20 min. Centering Prayer session

Assignment: Do Daily Activities for Chapter 3

Review practice, questions and reactions for follow up discussions next session

Daily Follow Up Activities

Chapter 3

Day 1 – List time and location of your centering prayer practice(s) today

Centering Prayer session # 1_____

Centering Prayer session # 2_____

*During the day, when you think about it, use the sacred word whenever you feel you should let something go.What happens as a result of doing this?

Day 2 - List time and location of your centering prayer practice(s) today

Centering Prayer session # 1_____

Centering Prayer session # 2_____

Take a few minutes to meditate on these words from Isaiah -

"...*I have formed you in your mother's womb...I have called you by name and you are mine*."

What thoughts arise, or feelings felt? Remember be honest, don't judge yourself.

What you feel, you feel. Only honesty is asked.

Day 3 –* List the time and location of your centering prayer practice(s) today

Centering Prayer session # 1_____

Centering Prayer session # 2_____

*Although we have no specific proof that Jesus prayed in silence, some examples from scripture as to how he prayed indicate what he did do.

 Read the following scriptures on how Jesus prayed, and list the things these descriptions had in common as to how Jesus prayed:

Mat 14:23

Mark 1:35

Luke 5:16

Luke 6:12

*How do these commonalities relate to the practice of Centering Prayer?

Day 4 - List the time and location of your centering prayer practice(s) today

Centering Prayer session # 1_____

Centering Prayer session # 2_____

Day 5 - List the time and location of your centering prayer practice(s) today

Centering Prayer session # 1_____

Centering Prayer session # 2_____

*Now that you have tried Centering Prayer daily for a week, what are some questions you have regarding the practice?

What are some obstacles you faced in trying to do the prayer?

CHAPTER 4

METHOD OF CENTERING PRAYER II

Now that you have spent the last week practicing Centering Prayer, it is time to address and share information regarding:

Questions regarding the Practice

Difficulties encountered during the practice this past week

Reactions to the practice this past week

Times used to Center

Locations used to Center

Close with 20 minute Centering Prayer Session

Complete activities for Chapter 4

Read Chapter 5

Daily Follow Up Activities

Chapter 4

Day 1 – List time and location of your centering prayer practice(s) today

Centering Prayer session # 1_____

Centering Prayer session # 2_____

Day 2 - List time and location of your centering prayer practice(s) today

Centering Prayer session # 1_____

Centering Prayer session # 2_____

Take a few minutes to meditate on these words from Isaiah -

Day 3 – List the time and location of your centering prayer practice(s) today

Centering Prayer session # 1_____

Centering Prayer session # 2_____

Day 4 – List the time and location of your centering prayer practice(s) today

Centering Prayer session # 1_____

Centering Prayer session # 2_____

Day 5 - List the time and location of your centering prayer practice(s) today

Centering Prayer session # 1_____

Centering Prayer session # 2_____

CHAPTER 5

THOUGHTS AND THE USE OF THE SACRED WORD

We now come to "Review Time."

The purpose of "review time" is so we can realize the subtle points of centering prayer, and come to a fuller understanding of what we're doing, and what God is accomplishing in us.

It's not difficult; it's like taking a clock apart to see what makes it tick.

So here goes:

1 Reread the Method of Centering Prayer Guidelines, and in particular, review Guideline#3 of the Method of Centering Prayer-"When engaged with your thoughts, return ever-so-gently to the sacred word."

A. The sacred word is a symbol that expresses our INTENTION and CONSENT to God's presence and action within. Each time we use our sacred word we are actually saying a small one word prayer to God that tells him of our intent to be in his presence and we give our consent for Him to act within us. What we must remember is that this word is sacred not because of what it may have come to mean, but because of the meaning WE give to it as the expression of our INTENTION and CONSENT. Got it?

We use the words God's PRESENCE and ACTION within. God's presence confirms our basic goodness, God's unconditional love. God's action is the healing process within. We cannot heal ourselves. We have tried so many times, in so many ways. Without God, we fail. God's actions within us can begin to heal us from the inside out. We must consent to God working within us.

B. The sacred word is not used when we notice thoughts going by, but when we're really and truly involved with these thought, when we begin "thinking " about the thoughts. Maybe an example might help:

 Think of our normal level of consciousness as a highway, and our thoughts are cars moving on that highway. We can have these thoughts, or cars, go by, sometimes many of them, and we just watch them go by. However if we notice one we like- say a red Chevy Corvette- and we stop it to look at it and admire it, looking inside the car, under the hood, etc. This is "thinking" about that thought- that car. We need to go back to our sacred word, and let the corvette go driving by. Anytime we come to realize that we become engaged in a thought, as described above…we return ever so gently to the sacred word.

C. In Centering Prayer both THOUGHTS and SILENCE have an important part to play. Some thoughts even need to be healed, believe it or not, and the silence creates a place for this to take place.

D. Each time we return to the sacred word is a prayer and an ACT of LOVE., because doing this tells God of our intention to consent to his presence. Amazing isn't it that such a tiny movement- the ONLY action we take in this prayer, can be a prayer and an act of love. God certainly doesn't want much, does He?

Definition of the term "Thoughts"

A. "Thoughts" is an umbrella term for any ideas at all, including images, emotions, memories, reflections, concepts, commentaries, and spiritual experiences.

B. Thoughts are going to happen . Our body breathes, our mind thinks. God does not want us to stop either.

In Centering Prayer, we do not eliminate thoughts, but expect them to come. We just want to try to slow down our thoughts. Some have expressed the fear that the Devil will come into our mind if we are in Centering Prayer. In response, Fr. Thomas Keating has this comment:

 "The devil cannot perceive what you are doing in centering prayer if it is deep enough. He can only know what is in your imagination and memory, and he can add material to these thoughts. But when you are in deep interior silence, what is happening there is God's secret. Only God knows what goes on in the depths. of the soul."

So whenever we find ourselves "thinking about our thoughts" instead of letting them go by, we go back to our sacred word.

Story

In one of the very earliest training workshops, led by Fr. Thomas Keating, a participant tried out her first 20 min. taste of Centering Prayer and then said " Oh Father Thomas, I'm such a failure at this prayer. In twenty minutes , I've had ten thousand thoughts." "How lovely!" responded Father Keating without missing a beat, " Ten thousand opportunities to return to God!"

THOUGHTS AND THE USE OF THE SACRED WORD

Kinds of Thoughts

A. Ordinary Wanderings of the imagination or memory

Outside noises- door clanging, announcements, people moving. Thoughts about what you were doing just prior to prayer-working, reading, moving from area to area, in the chow hall, discussions, etc.. These are noises you are aware of in your everyday life in this environment. Treat them as background music in a store- try to ignore them and gradually you will develop the capacity to pay no attention to them. Go ever so gently back to your sacred word

B. Thoughts that give rise to likes or dislikes

These are thoughts that bring good feelings or feelings of strong emotions, both good and bad. These thoughts bring up strong likes or dislikes. Go ever so gently back to your sacred word.

C. Insights

In the quiet, we might think we have come up with new solutions to big problems, clarification of prior difficulties with family or friends, new insights into your incarceration, answers to questions we have had, religious revelations, etc.. Go ever so gently back to your sacred word.

D. Self-reflections

Here we may have thoughts such as " I wonder if I am doing this prayer right?' or "I think I am really getting it now…." All these are still thoughts. Go back to your sacred word.

E. Thoughts arising from the unconscious

These may begin early in our practice: feelings and thoughts that we are not sure where they come from. This process of unconscious thoughts coming to us is known as the healing action of the Holy Spirit.

Remember what St. Paul said:

> *"…when the Lord comes, He will bring to light what is hidden in the darkness and will manifest the motives of our hearts…"*(1Cor:4:5)

Remember the 3 R's when we were kids? Well, now with regard to our thoughts we remember the 4 R's

The 4 R's

***Resist** no thought

***Retain** no thought

***React** emotionally to no thought

***Return** ever-so-gently to the Sacred Word when engaged with your thoughts.

Centering Prayer is a method not a "technique". It is a method of allowing ourselves to be transformed from the inside. Therefore during this prayer we avoid analyzing our experience, having expectations, or aiming at some specific goal such as:

*Repeating the sacred word continuously

*Having no thoughts

*Making the mind a blank

*Feeling peaceful or consoled

*Achieving a spiritual experience

A Yearning for God

In all of us there's a deep yearning or desire for God. And whether we know it or not, we've had it since the day we were born but most of us don't recognize it as such.

When we begin a prayer like Centering prayer this yearning increases and increases to the point that we can't help but desire God more and more. And so we might have thoughts like, "Am I doing this prayer right?" or "I don't feel God's presence!" or even, "My sacred word is not working!"

In other words, we have expectations, and when we do, we must recognize this as an attempt to control our relationship with God. We have to remember that the Intention and Consent of our will (heart) does, without doubt, open us to the divine presence and action within. God is working and present to us at the deepest level of our being. We can't see or feel this because we haven't the ability. We must trust in pure faith. This doesn't sound very encouraging, but by doing so we're maturing, we're growing up in our faith so as to meet the living God, and in so doing, becoming stronger in our intimate relationship with Him.

THOUGHTS AND THE USE OF THE SACRED WORD

Again, St. Paul's words –

"In the same way, the Spirit too comes to the aid of our weakness; for we do not know how to pray as we ought, but the Spirit itself intercedes with sighs too deep for words."

(Romans 8:26)

The Practice

A. The intention and consent to God's presence and action are the heart and soul of the centering prayer practice.

B. When engaged with your thoughts, return ever-so gently to the sacred word

C. By "returning-ever-so-gently to the sacred word", a minimum of effort is indicated. This is the only activity we initiate during the time of Centering Prayer

D. Once you grasp the fact that thoughts are not only unavoidable but an necessary part of the process of healing and growth initiated by God, you will be able to take a friendlier attitude towards them.

E. Progress in Centering Prayer does not eliminate thoughts, but leads to a lack of connection from all thoughts. Discipline in Centering Prayer is indicated by the promptness with which you return to the sacred word when engaged in thoughts. This is the discipline of Centering Prayer- not disciplining yourself to do it, but disciplining yourself to go to your sacred word whenever you begin to engage your thoughts.

F. Thoughts do not interrupts this prayer unless you get up and walk out or deliberately get involved them.

Finally, a statement from Fr. Thomas Keating:

"The sacred word is a way of letting go of all thoughts. This makes it possible for our spiritual faculties, which are attracted to interior silence, to move spontaneously in that direction. Such a movement does not require effort. It only requires the willingness to let go of our ordinary preoccupations."

*Close with 20 min. Centering Prayer Session

Assignment: Do Daily Activities for Chapter 5

Read Chapter 6 for next class

Daily Follow Up Activities

Chapter 5

Day 1 – List time and location of your centering prayer practice(s) today

Centering Prayer session # 1_____

Centering Prayer session # 2_____

*How does the use of the sacred word help you in this prayer?

Day 2 - * List the time and location of your centering prayer practice(s) today

Centering Prayer session # 1_____

Centering Prayer session # 2 _____

*We usually understand the word "thoughts" in a specific way. But in Centering Prayer the word "thoughts" is broader. Reflecting on your current environment, give some examples of this.

Day 3-* List the time and location of your centering prayer practice(s) today

Centering Prayer session # 1_____

Centering Prayer session # 2 _____

*There are all kinds of "thoughts"-ordinary wanderings, thoughts that attract or repel us, insights that give us new knowledge, self-reflections , and thoughts arising form the unconscious. Which of these do you think occurs more often than others in your periods of centering prayer? Which do you think occur less often? Do you get a sense of why ?

Day 4 - *List the time and location of your centering prayer practice(s) today

Centering Prayer session # 1_____

Centering Prayer session # 2_____

*St. Paul said ***"…when the Lord comes, He will bring to light what is hidden in the darkness and will manifest the motives of our hearts***…" (1Cor 4:5) Do you agree with St. Paul? Explain

THOUGHTS AND THE USE OF THE SACRED WORD

Day 5-* List the time and location of your centering prayer practice(s) today

Centering Prayer session # 1_____

Centering Prayer session # 2 _____

*In Centering Prayer we are not supposed to have any expectations. In your current environment, you may find this is very hard to do. What are some expectations individuals sharing this environment may have during this prayer?

CHAPTER 6

LECTIO DIVINA

Lectio Divina. What is this? Are these words? Yes, they're Latin words and they mean sacred (divina) reading (lectio) of Scripture.

Throughout the centuries, as well as today, monks in monasteries have participated in this sacred reading of Scripture. It was their way of getting closer to Christ and deepening their relationship with him. What better way was there than to read in the Bible what he had to say, or see what he did, how he lived, whom he spent time with, how he spoke to others, how he loved, and how he died.

Through this sacred reading Jesus became alive for these monks. His presence was felt everywhere, in all that they did, in people they saw, books they read, and in the performance of their daily duties. It was as if Jesus jumped out of the Scriptures just to walk beside them.

Before the printing press was invented, monks had to listen to the words of Scripture, and learn them by heart so that they could pray with them throughout the day. They repeatedly whispered the words so that even their bodies were engaged in conversation with the living God. The monks would also read very slowly, the whole process of Lectio Divina taking at times a couple of hours each day. Today this sacred reading continues to be one of the most important things a monk can do.

In our day we're so overwhelmed with newspapers, magazines, and other reading materials that we tend to look at the Bible as just another book that needs to be read. Far from it! It's just the opposite! The Bible needs to be tasted, reflected upon, regarded as a living thing that speaks to us lovingly, and holds secrets for us personally, as well as that which holds the seeds of friendship with Christ.

Believe it or not, Lectio Divina is also a form of contemplative prayer. The reason we can say this is that when we read Scripture, we're doing it not for information but for insight. It's not to learn something, but to meet Christ. A friendship is developing. And as the process unfolds we recognize (as we do in centering prayer) that the word of God is within us, not like some statue, but rather as something living and very much a part of our lives.

Centering prayer helps us to "listen" to the word of God within us by being immersed in the silence. Lectio Divina helps us to "listen" to the word of God within us by listening to the words of Scripture. For each of us the experience is different, because we have a

God who speaks to us according to who we are regardless of our lives, past or present. How could it be otherwise?

So let's take this gift that's been given us and see how it works.

Four Stages of Lectio Divina

Today, we practice Lectio Divina as a four step discipline built around the practice of reading scripture:

The first stage is lectio(reading) It directs us to carefully listen as we read the scriptures.

(Like reading a letter for information)

The second stage is meditatio(meditation)- this second stage is activity of the mind, determining the meaning of and application to the text to our lives.

(Like reading a letter from a loved one, where we read beyond the words to what the words really mean us)

The third stage is Oratio (prayer) prayer as the turning of the heart to God to get what we need from him. It is praying from and through our hearts.

(We leave the mind and go to the heart. We discuss our perceptions and desires with God who loves us most. We now speak back to God what He has spoken to us)

The fourth stage is contemplatio (contemplation) This means we've come to the point where we can rest in the Word of God. We also rest in the arms of God. Now that we've prayed to him through Scripture using words and images that come to our minds, now, we can let aall that go and simply rest in his love.

An example from Mother Theresa's life may help illustrate what this means:

A pilgrim once asked Mother Theresa, "Mother, how do you pray?"

Mother Theresa replied, " I close my eyes and pray in silence."

Puzzled, the pilgrim asked, "What are you doing while your eyes are closed?"

"I am listening to God," replied Mother Theresa.

Still confused, the pilgrim asked," and what do you suppose God is doing all this time?"

To which she replied, "He is listening to me."

We can let the words and images go, and simply feel. Feel loved by God, caressed by his as a Father caresses his infant son. And if, for whatever reason, we can't feel his love, then believe, in faith, that this is what's happening. Sooner or later God will allow you to feel his love. He can't help; it since he's love itself.

Listen to those words in Scripture that are repeated time and time again, "Do not be afraid," "Fear not."

For the practice of underline personal Lectio Divina, you can stop during your reading when a part of scripture interests you and use that scripture selection for personal Lectio Divina, or you can go to a familiar piece of scripture to use for personal Lectio Divina or you can choose a piece of scripture to read for any reason you feel called.

PERSONAL LECTIO DIVINA

1-Very slowly, read a small portion of Scripture.(lectio)

2-Ask what it calls you to? What thought or feeling, conviction or intention arises in you because of it? (meditatio)

3-Share all this with God in your own heartfelt words (this is prayer as relationship!) (Oratio)

4- Rest in God (Contemplatio) Rest in the presence of the living Word of God.

Quote from Guigo the Carthusian

"Reading is the foundation and comes first. It supplies material and then refers us to meditation. Meditation earnestly inquires what we should seek and as it were, digs out and finds the treasures and shows us the treasures. But since it cannot obtain anything by itself,(because the head can never get us where we want to go), it refers us to prayer. Prayer raises itself up with all its might toward God and asks for the desired treasure, the sweetness of contemplation. This, when it comes, rewards the labors of the preceding three."

Toward Resting In God

Fr. Carl Arico, who wrote extensively on Lectio Divina, states:

"What is beneficial about the process of Lectio Divina is that one can move from one level of relating to Jesus to the next in the same period of prayer, experiencing a variety of responses .and gradually as a friendship with Jesus

deepens, the "four senses of scripture" begin to unfold as a dynamic within one's own life."

The method of Lectio Divina is similar to the pattern we use in getting to know someone. The following chart will show this pattern.

Toward Resting in God

Prayer as Relationship	Lectio Divina
Acquaintanceship	Reading
Friendliness	Reflection
Friendship	Spontaneous Prayer
Intimacy	Resting in God
	Contemplation

What moves us from one level to another? Is it something we do? In the method of Lectio Divina, we just keep reading the Scriptures, and listening to the word of God. Eventually we will begin to grow in our understanding of the role of scripture plays in our lives and we will be helped in continuing on our Spiritual Journey.

We need all four steps as we progress on our journey, even though it seems at times that we may be emphasizing only one of them For example, there are times when we may be more interested in the reading; sometimes we may find ourselves more involved in reflection. Often prayer seems to be the most important activity for us, and at other times resting in God attracts us. All four steps are always there, and we need all four for real nourishment. If we are aware of the whole process being present, then the prayer will be positive and spirit filled.

Another Quote from Guigo the Carthusian

"Reading without meditation is arid. Meditation without reading is erroneous. Prayer without meditation is tepid. Meditation without prayer is fruitless. Prayer with devotion wins contemplation, but the attainment of contemplation without prayer is rare and miraculous."

Group Lectio Divina

Although Lectio Divina is usually seen as an individual prayer practice, many involved in Contemplation and Centering prayer find that doing group Lectio Divina during group centering prayer meetings, is a very powerful use of the prayer.

LECTIO DIVINA

Shared in Community

LECTIO

Reading God's Word

1. <u>One person reads aloud (twice)</u> the passage of scripture as others are attentive to some segment that is especially meaningful to them.

2. Short silence… Each hears and silently repeats a word or phrase that attracts them.

3. Sharing aloud: each person repeats out loud the word or phrase that has spoken to them or attracted them.(No elaboration)

MEDITATIO

Reflection on God's Word

4. <u>Second reading</u> of the same passage by another person.

5. Short silence…Reflect on "Where does the content of this touch my life today?

6. Sharing aloud: Briefly share what the reading means to you?: "I hear, I see, I was struck by…"

ORATIO

Responding to God

7. <u>Third reading</u> by still another person

8. Short silence…Reflect on how God is calling me to respond

9. Sharing aloud: Briefly pray spontaneously expressing hour response to God's call

CONTEMPLATIO

Resting in God

10. Fourth Reading by another person

11. Rest in the Word in silence.

12. Allow the Word to do whatever needs to be done so that we can become more of what God wants us to be.

*Close with a 20 min. Centering Prayer session group and Lectio Divina,

Assignment: Do Daily Activities for Chapter 6

Read Content of Chapter 7 for next class

Daily Follow Up Activities

Chapter 6

Day 1 – List time and location of your centering prayer practice(s) today

Centering Prayer session # 1_____

Centering Prayer session # 2_____

*List the scripture used for your personal Lectio Divina practice_____

*When doing Lectio Divina did you get a sense of what Jesus might be saying toyou?

What seems to be coming through? Trust yourself on this one, especially your feelings.

Day 2 - List time and location of your centering prayer practice(s) today

Centering Prayer session # 1_____

Centering prayer session # 2 _____

*List the scripture used for your personal Lectio Divina practice_____

* What is it that you like about Lectio Divina? What is it that you dislike? List them

Day 3- List the time and location of your centering prayer practice)s) today:

Centering Prayer session # 1_____

Centering Prayer session # 2_____

*List the scripture used for your personal Lectio Divina practice_____

*Reflect on this quote:

"When I do Lectio Divina, the barriers of time and this prison I am in, disappear. I seem to be back in Nazareth or Galilee or Jerusalem with Jesus, or Jesus is here with me right where I am, even in this place, here in the present moment. Either way it happens, everything else seems to fade away."

LECTIO DIVINA

Day 4 - *List the time and location of your centering prayer practice(s) today

      Centering Prayer session # 1_____

      Centering Prayer session # 2_____

*List the scripture used for your personal Lectio Divina practice_____

*From what you've read so far while doing Lectio Divina, can you identify with any of the characters in scripture? And if you can, then ask yourself-am I like this person?   What does he (or she) look like? Do I feel the way he (or she) feels? If I had a chance, what would I say to him(or her)? Do I see them in any of the inmates I see everyday here?

Day 5 - List the time and location of your centering prayer practice(s) today

      Centering Prayer session # 1_____

      Centering Prayer session # 2_____

*List the scripture used for your personal Lectio Divina practice_____

*In Scripture, read about the last days of Jesus' life. Is his suffering in some way like your suffering? Is Jesus' suffering continuing now in your suffering?

(Remember that you're not separate from him. We only think we are).

Suggested readings: MAT 26-27, or MARK 14-5, or LUKE 22-23 or JOHN 11-19

CHAPTER 7

<u>DEEPENING OUR RELATIONSHIP WITH GOD</u>

Make no doubt about it – we were made in the image and likeness of God. No matter who we are or what we've done, or whether we believe it or not, our fundamental goodness exists!

Remember the Book of Genesis?

   "So God created humankind in God's image, in the image of God, God created them; male and female God created them." (Genesis 1:27)

Our fundamental goodness is a necessary element of Christian faith. This basic core of goodness is our true Self, who we are in the eyes of God, not who we think we are.

The acceptance of our basic goodness (when we finally get around to accepting it) is really a quantum leap in our spiritual journey.

Not only this, but our basic core of goodness is capable of unlimited, yes, unlimited development, much like being transformed into Christ.

Within the culture that we live, many people, in fact, the majority of people have a poor self-image. It's almost impossible not to have one. The media and some of the values we hold, plus the way we've been raised, all contribute to this image of ourselves. On top of this we have feelings of guilt, fear, anger, unworthiness, whether conscious or unconscious. These things do not make for good relationships. But, by being faithful to the practice of Centering Prayer, one relationship definitely deepens, and this is our relationship to Christ. And as this deepens, all the obstacles we've given both to ourselves and others will gradually disappear.

There will be greater space for God to enter and fill us with His love.

As John The Baptist said, "***He (Jesus) must increase and I must decrease.***"(John 3:30)

One funny thing about this prayer: Other people will notice the changes in us before we do.

Another thing – in some mysterious way – we'll have a greater understanding of the needs of the human family and we'll respond to others with greater compassion and mercy. We'll be able to carry out Christ's words when he said:

"Amen, I say to you, whatever you did for one of these least brothers (and sisters) of mine, you did for me." (Mt.25:40)

Another funny thing about this prayer: We can't judge how we're doing this prayer, not by our psychological experiences, or our physical sensations, or the time we put into it, or by comparing our prayer with others! Only God can judge because only He knows what's really happening on the deepest level of this prayer!

THE HOLY SPIRIT

Now we come to the Holy Spirit. The Spirit's inspiration may be expressed in a number of ways:

A. Need of silence in one's life-turning of the radio more often, not listening to outside conversations

B. An ability to "let go" in daily life- Arguing less, getting less stressed and upset

C.A growing capacity to listen- not just to others, but to scripture as well

D.A non-judgmental attitude begins to develop toward ourselves and others- greater acceptance of those that are different from us. They become different, not deficient!

E .Learning to be open to give and to receive. We begin to live the Benedictine welcome: *"Come right in and disturb our lives- you are the Christ for us today."*

F .Our prayer life becomes richer – we seek out bible study, prayer groups and discussions

G. Growth in self-knowledge, which may be painful-We understand our false self and our strengths

H. Respect for other religions and sacred traditions- We are less biased against and closed to faith journeys of others

I. Practical caring for others and for all Creation.- Reaching out to those who need us here in this environment with in our families and friends

J.A growing awareness of the social application of the Gospel. Reaching out to others with your faith. Doing good works based on the scriptures.

Practical Ways to Deepen Our Relationship With God

*Practice two sessions of Centering Prayer daily

*Read scripture with more meaning, using personal Lectio Divina

*Attempt to meet with others for group centering and lectio opportunities

Quote on Group meetings for Centering Prayer:

"In contemplative practice, as we pray together, we believe that Christ is in the center of the circle imparting to each the special graces each one needs. The participants are pooling their silence, so to speak, so that everyone gathered there can drink from this marvelous well of living water that rises up form the center of the circle. Silence in this context is liturgy of an exalted kind. We do not say or do anything, but we engage in a special kind of action that might be called alert receptivity. It is opening and consenting to God's presence and action within us.

It is here people are struggling to move through the traditional stages of the spiritual journey and are supported by the presence, example, prayers and wisdom of like-minded companions or soul-friends."

Thomas Keating "The Better Part"

And as we mature in this practice, our ability to live in the present moment develops and grows.

But – most important of all:

The purpose of this practice of Centering Prayer is so that one day we might achieve the Contemplative state which is not a series of experiences, however great these might be, but rather a permanent and abiding awareness of God all the time, in all that we do, or say, or give. We become like a Fifth Gospel in which our lives may be the only Gospel some people may ever read.

* Close the class with a 20 min. Centering Prayer Session group and Lectio Divina

Assignment: Do Daily Activities for Chapter 7

Read the content for Chapter 8 for next class

Daily Follow Up Activities

Chapter 7

Day 1 – List time and location of your centering prayer practice(s) today

      Centering Prayer session # 1_____

      Centering Prayer session # 2_____

*List the scripture used for your personal Lectio Divina practice_____

*Do you believe, without qualification, that at the core of our being people are fundamentally good? Explain

Day 2 - List time and location of your centering prayer practice(s) today

      Centering Prayer session # 1_____

      Centering Prayer session # 2 _____

*List the scripture used for your personal Lectio Divina practice_____

* What makes it difficult for some to believe in the fundamental goodness of man?

Day 3- * List the time and location of your centering prayer practice(s) today

      Centering Prayer session # 1_____

      Centering Prayer session # 2 _____

*List the scripture used for your personal Lectio Divina practice_____

*Does God feel our pain, our guilt, fear, anger, unworthiness? And, if so, God, in some mysterious way, suffers with us. God is in our suffering. Talk with God about this.

Day 4 -   *List the time and location of your centering prayer practice(s) today

      Centering Prayer session # 1_____

      Centering Prayer session # 2_____

*List the scripture used for your personal Lectio Divina practice_____

*Being human, we're forever judging ourselves and others even though Jesus asks us not to do so. What harm may we be doing ourselves if we do judge ourselves?

Day 5 - *List the time and location of your centering prayer practice(s) today

      Centering Prayer session # 1_____

      Centering Prayer session # 2_____

*List the scripture used for your personal Lectio Divina practice_____

One of the inspirations of the Holy Spirit is a growing awareness of the social application of the Gospel(it's relationship to our daily lives with others).

Reflect on what this can mean to you personally.

CHAPTER 8

THE FRUITS OF CENTERING PRAYER

We get presents from the Holy Spirit. They are called the fruits of the Holy Spirit.

There's no direct cause and effect connection between Centering Prayer and the fruits of the Spirit, but let's face it, if we're doing Centering Prayer and our relationship with God

deepens as a result, transformation will be noticed in our lives. And when transformation

occurs, those fruits will be there. It can't be otherwise. That's just the way it is.

"...The Fruits of the Spirit are indications of God's presence at work in us at varying degrees and forms. Through the Fruits, the Spirit is becoming a reality in our lives."

Fr. Thomas Keating "The Gifts of the Holy Spirit"

And according to St. Paul –

"...The Spirit produces love, joy, peace, patience, kindness, goodness, faithfulness, gentleness, and self-control." (Galatians 5:22)

So, expect these fruits. You'll receive them without your even noticing.

Let's take a look at them:

The first three are in relationship with God

Love – When we love, truly love, even though our love may be limited, we are actually participating in God's unconditional love. Hard to believe, isn't it? Yet God wants nothing less but for us to do this.

Joy – is an ever present sense of well-being because we have a relationship with God.

Joy is more than being happy. It is quiet, gentle, and, unlike happiness that can come and go, joy remains with us at a deep level.

Peace – is a sense of comfort that comes from being rooted in God, while at the same time being more and more aware of our nothingness (nothingness, that is, compared to God).

The next three are in relationship with others

Patience - (long suffering) is being completely certain of God's unfailing faithfulness to us and to His promises, even though on the surface it may sometimes seem otherwise.

Kindness - (meekness) is freedom from the energy of hatred or outbursts of anger. (This doesn't mean we go around like doormats or victims, but the energy required for deep hatred and anger is gone).

Goodness – is the affirmation of creation as good, together with a sense of oneness with the universe and with everything created.

The final three are in relationship with ourselves

Faithfulness – is the daily offering of ourselves and all our actions to God as well as showing compassion for others, especially in service to their real needs.

Gentleness – is doing things God's way, a way that is at once gentle and firm, that recognizes the differences in all of creation, yet doing it all without effort.

Self-Control – is not using our will to control our emotions, but rather a fruit that arises spontaneously because of our ever-deepening relationship with God.

Back to St. Paul who says:

> *"If anyone is in Christ, he or she is a new creature."*(2 Cor 5:17)

And so, as a result of Centering Prayer, we not only have the **fruits** of the Spirit, but the **gifts** as well.

These **gifts** are the result of the Holy Spirit purifying us in both our conscious and unconscious reasons for doing what we do and being who we are. Purifying here means that ever-so-gently the Spirit is bringing us to freedom, freedom from the forces inside us that drive us to do, or to be, what we don't want.

The gifts of knowledge, understanding & wisdom:

These three gifts overlap quite a bit, and if one gift grows, the others do too.

These three gifts are God's way of grabbing our entire being so that the whole of us may belong to God: body, mind, and spirit.

Knowledge: The gift of knowledge helps us to see that the way we view the world may be unreal, and that our way of looking at life is not the only way.

THE FRUITS OF CENTERING PRAYER

According to Fr. Thomas Keating:

"...God is extremely down to earth and has a sense of humor and playfulness, qualities that Jesus manifests in the Gospels especially in the parables."

Understanding The gift of understanding gives us not ordinary thoughts but rather spiritual impressions or insights that arise spontaneously. It gives us a realistic view of our own weaknesses.

Wisdom   The gift of wisdom allows us to see as God sees. It gives us a kind of divine vision into events and it allows us to "see" the Divine Presence and action at work, even in very tragic and painful situations.

Then there are the gifts of reverence, fortitude, piety, and counsel:

These four gifts help us to carry the experience of Centering Prayer into daily life, that is, in our dealing with others.

Reverence: The gift of reverence causes us to realize that our lives are unmanageable without the grace of God.

Fortitude: The gift of fortitude gives us the energy to overcome major difficulties in our spiritual growth.

Piety : The gift of piety softens the sense of reverence for God and over-strictness with ourselves. It also helps us to see others as companions on the journey rather than competitors.

Counsel: The gift of counsel helps us to see what our long-range plans should be as well how to manage the details of daily life. The more open we are to the Spirit, the more the Spirit will take over our lives. The Spirit will even lead our lives for us. We make mistakes but keep coming back to the realization that God knows how to live our lives. Only god knows the long road. Only his plans for us are going to work, not ours.

With the gifts & fruits of the Spirit, life is turned around for us. We're able finally to see, both in sorrow and in joy, the unfailing love of God for us, and His promise of eternal life.

Most important of all: **The conviction of being greatly loved by God grows through these seven gifts.**

It may be very hard to see the change within you. We are so accustomed to being the way we've been, it's hard to believe God's power is actually changing us. But look closely at yourself, try to recognize where the lord has improved upon you. Recognize his gifts within you.

* Close class with 20 min. Centering Prayer Session group and Lectio Divina

Assignment- Do daily activities for Chapter 8

Read Chapter 9 content

Daily Follow Up Activities

Chapter 8

Day 1 – *List the time and location of your centering prayer practice(s) today

      Centering Prayer session # 1_____

      Centering Prayer session # 2_____

*List the scripture used for your personal Lectio Divina practice_____

When we do a practice like Centering Prayer we open up to God, true, but God opens up to us so much more. An example is the fruits and gifts we receive from the Holy Spirit. What do you think happens to us when we receive these fruits and gifts?

Day 2-*List the time and location of your centering prayer practice(s) today

      Centering Prayer session # 1_____

      Centering Prayer session # 2_____

*List the scripture used for your personal Lectio Divina practice_____

*Nothing can harm us if we have the peace that is rooted in God. If we are not referring to physical harem how can this apply to your life in your current environment right now?

Day 3-*List the time and location of your centering prayer practice(s) today

      Centering Prayer session # 1_____

      Centering Prayer session # 2_____

*List the scripture used for your personal Lectio Divina practice_____

* The spiritual journey is not all sweetness and light. Sometimes, it asks hard things of us. What gift can we ask for to help us? How can this gift help you daily within the current environment you now live in with those with whom you live?

Day 4 -   *List the time and location of your centering prayer practice(s) today

    Centering Prayer session # 1_____

    Centering Prayer session # 2_____

*List the scripture used for your personal Lectio Divina practice_____

Fr. Thomas tells us that God, among many things, is playful. What are the things in all of creation that reveals God's playfulness to you?

Day 5 - List the time and location of your centering prayer practice(s) today

    Centering Prayer session # 1_____

    Centering Prayer session # 2_____

*List the scripture used for your personal Lectio Divina practice_____

*Take a person who is in your current environment that you have a lot of contact with and try to see him as God sees him.What happens? Do you feel differently about that person? Would you act differently toward that person?

CHAPTER 9

EXTENDING THE FRUITS OF CENTERING PRAYER INTO DAILY LIFE & THE FUTURE

ACTIVE PRAYER

Don't let the long title of this chapter throw you off. It's not as confusing as it looks.

This chapter introduces us to the first of three spiritual practices that can help us with various things that pop up in our lives, as well as help keep our awareness of the presence of God close to us each moment of the day. You might think to yourselves, "What, three more practices?" It's not as complicated as it might seem at first. You might also ask yourselves, "Why? Why do we need these when we already have centering prayer and lectio? Isn't this enough?

Well, in a way it is, but if we want to become aware of the presence of God every minute, these practices are mini-gold mines. You see by keeping our awareness of God steady like this over the course of time, suddenly one day that awareness will turn into a reality. And when that happens everything is transformed! We may be in the most horrible conditions but to us it will seem like paradise because we will know with every bone in our bodies that we don't want or need anything else. What we have attained is heaven on earth.

Ready?

The Active Prayer

The first practice is called the Active Prayer. The Active Prayer is an ancient practice that, like all contemplative practices such as Centering Prayer and Lectio Divina, purposefully brings our awareness into the divine presence of God. It is a way of praying every minute. It is an attempt to do what St. Paul encouraged in his letter to the Thessalonians 5:17

"We should pray without ceasing with each breath and heartbeat of our being"

Active prayer, like any contemplative method that seeks modification of thoughts, whets our desire throughout the day for prayer in silence- to rest in the intimacy of God's abiding presence. It is used outside of Centering Prayer during our ordinary activities.

It's usually said while you're not concentrating on something where you have to be really focused. For example, if we're doing a really boring job like scrubbing the floor, this doesn't take much attention or concentration, right? Well, why not say a few words that are really a prayer while we're scrubbing the floor? It won't take anything away from scrubbing the floor, but it will keep us aware of the presence of God while we're doing it.

Or, what if we have to stuff envelopes or work on a factory line? Let's face it, work like this doesn't require us to concentrate. These kinds of jobs are pretty boring. So it's the perfect time to use this active prayer. Guaranteed the work will seem less boring, and we're sure to be touched by God in new ways.

The important thing is to keep it simple, but keep it real!

This life is filled with menial chores we are required to do every day. You hear people all around you complaining and whining about what they are doing. Wouldn't it be great to turn those menial chores into an opportunity to communicate with God?

1. Choose a six to twelve syllable sentence, and keep repeating it to yourself and to God.

For example,

> "Oh, Lord, come to my assistance."
>
> "God help me to trust always in you."
>
> "Lord, help me keep true to myself."
>
> "Lord, teach me patience."
>
> "Lord, change my hatred to love."
>
> "Speak Lord, your servant is listening."
>
> "Jesus, help me to see the good in all."
>
> "Jesus, have mercy on me, your beloved sinner."

Feel free to make up whatever you like. But make sure that whatever you make up expresses a desire for something personal in your relationship with God, and, above all, have it MEAN SOMETHING TO YOU. Don't make up something nice because you think it's nice for God. More than anything else God wishes us to be honest with Him and with ourselves.

Another thing – by repeating this prayer over and over for days, weeks, months, the prayer, in some mysterious way, becomes a part of us. It gets lodged deep inside us, deep enough so that we'll never be the same again. The practice of Active Prayer interrupts and erases the intensity of our interior dialogue. It is then that God takes center stage.

2. Above all, don't rush it and say it without worry. This prayer is said <u>without</u> **anxiety, haste** or **effort**. Everything we do for God is done easily; we flow with it, are peaceful with it and are joyful with it. Like centering prayer, we just do it. As long as we're sincere, God will do the rest. If you're mind wanders while saying the prayer, you gently return to the words as we return to the sacred word in centering prayer.

There may come a time when you feel that the words you've selected no longer hold much energy for you. Or you find yourself in a situation where you'd like to change the words so that they'll express what you might be going through at a particular time.

Yes, you may change the words of the prayer to suit you at that time. Just ask Jesus to help you come up with some new words. Don't sweat it. Again, God accepts all we give him. The one thing He doesn't want you to have is anxiety over this or any other prayer, or for that matter, anything!

3. This prayer helps keep us in the same state we are in when we finish Centering Prayer or Lectio Divina. But it does more. What we ask for in this prayer will be given over time. Trust this. It's true.

Remember that the reason for this prayer is to keep our awareness of God present in all that we do, but that the best time to do it is when we have a job that requires little concentration.

Outside of jobs, we can also say this prayer if we're waiting on line for food, or waiting to take a shower, or even waiting for an appointment or a meeting or a class. So often we may have thoughts that make us angry or sad or anxious because our minds wander faster than bees around a honeycomb. The active prayer will rid us of anger, sadness, anxiety, or whatever negative thought we might have. It will calm our minds and help us to hold words that give meaning to our lives. This prayer also centers us which means that we will see things more clearly and from different perspectives.

And, let's face it, taking on more perspectives serves to establish peace, not only within ourselves but also in the world.

Close with a 20 min. Centering Prayer session Group and Lectio Divina

Assignment- Do activities for Chapter 9

Read Chapter 10 for next class

Daily Follow Up Activities

Chapter 9

Day 1-- List time and location of your centering prayer practice(s) today

      Centering Prayer session # 1_____

      Centering Prayer session # 2_____

*List the scripture used for your personal Lectio Divina practice_____

*Practice the Active Prayer as often as possible- write down your active prayer

_____

Day 2-- List time and location of your centering prayer practice(s) today

      Centering Prayer session # 1_____

      Centering Prayer session # 2_____

*List the scripture used for your personal Lectio Divina practice_____

*Practice the Active Prayer as often as possible

Day 3-- List time and location of your centering prayer practice(s) today

      Centering Prayer session # 1_____

      Centering Prayer session # 2_____

*List the scripture used for your personal Lectio Divina practice_____

*Practice the Active Prayer as often as possible

Day 4-- List time and location of your centering prayer practice(s) today

      Centering Prayer session # 1_____

      Centering Prayer session # 2_____

*List the scripture used for your personal Lectio Divina practice_____

*Practice the Active Prayer as often as possible

EXTENDING THE FRUITS OF CENTERING PRAYER
INTO DAILY LIFE & THE FUTURE

Day 5-– List time and location of your centering prayer practice(s) today

Centering Prayer session # 1_____

Centering Prayer session # 2_____

*List the scripture used for your personal Lectio Divina practice_____

*Practice the Active Prayer as often as possible

CHAPTER 10

EXTENDING THE FRUITS OF CENTERING PRAYER INTO DAILY LIFE & THE FUTURE

THE WELCOMING PRAYER

This prayer requires a bit of an explanation. We need to understand where we're coming from when we say this prayer, or it becomes just so many words without meaning.

Let's go back to when we were born.

First of all, we're born with certain genes that give us a particular temperament, physical characteristics, and many more qualities from parents and grandparents, and so on. Whether we like it or not, these remain with us for a lifetime.

As we grow older we experience different environments. We may come from dysfunctional families, orphanages, foster parents, gone to good schools or bad, come into good company or bad, had lots of money or had to earn it, fell in love or had our hearts broken. All these influences, and more besides, caused us to take many turns in life bringing us to the point where we are now. We reacted to them in ways resulting from our genes, influences, and free will.

What psychology found to be true over the years is that if a child's needs aren't satisfied when they're young, he/she will grow into an adult who demands these needs to be satisfied.

These needs revolve around what we'll call three nerve centers:

The need for security and survival.

The need for affection, esteem, and approval.

The need for power and control.

If these needs weren't satisfied when we were young, the adult in us wants them all the more and generally we will go to any length to satisfy them.

Let's look at an example:

A little child's need for security and survival was never satisfied. He grows up with one thought in mind. Make lots of money. So, as an adult he makes money, but it's never enough. He may be worth a lot but it's never enough. He never feels secure enough. He's over-identified with this need.

Or take a child who never felt affection or esteem. She realizes she has some talent so she decides to become a movie star. She wins award after award and still is unhappy, is never satisfied because the esteem and affection she gets from her public is not enough. She's over-identified with her need for affection, esteem and approval.

And the need for power and control? This is a big one. We see it all around us.

A person who never feels in control, or feels he cannot influence others, is over-identified with the center of power and control. He may join a gang in order to gain some power, or he may be one who never allows his wife or children the freedom to be who they are. He has to have control over their lives. Only he can do things right, only he knows what's right to think and believe. If control is taken from him, he feels useless, worthless.

He's over-identified with the power and control center.

What's important to remember is that these needs are not bad. We all need security, affection, and control. It's our **over-identification with these needs** that make us do all sorts of things that we wouldn't do otherwise, and to feel what we wouldn't feel otherwise. What's even more important to remember is that we don't realize this consciously. **This over-identification is unconscious.**

We're not aware that we're over-identifying with anything. We simply think this is the way we are.

But it's this over-identification with one or more of these nerve centers that causes us to blow up, or get angry, or appear helpless, or experience any number of things. After we leave Centering Prayer we may feel good, **but things happen on a daily basis** that get us all riled up and when this occurs we can be sure we've over-identified with one or more of the nerve centers.

This over-identification can only be taken away by God. We can't do it.

These needs are too deeply buried in our unconscious; we can't get at them, only God can.

And so we use the spiritual practice known as **The Welcoming Prayer.**

WELCOMING PRAYER

It goes like this:

The first thing we do when we become upset or someone sets something off in us is to **focus in on our body and try to locate where in our body this emotion or feeling is present. Once we've located the area, we sink into it.**

(Remember that in each cell of our body is contained every experience we've ever had.)

As we sink into the feeling we say to the Holy Spirit:

Welcome, Welcome, Welcome,

I let go of my desire for security (or survival).

I let go of my desire for affection (or esteem or approval).

I let go of my desire for control (or power).

I let go of my desire to change the present situation.

We don't repress anything in this prayer. Rather, we let it all go and have the Holy Spirit take over. Each time we do the prayer the over-identification with any of the nerve centers become less and less. At some point we'll find we have let go of our desire for control, or affection, or security. It'll happen over time without our being aware that it's happening, and one day we'll wake up to find that we no longer **identify** with these desires. They've become greatly diminished. They will no longer control us; we'll be free.

Let's review:

Become aware that you're upset

Locate where this feeling is in your body and sink into it

Say to the Spirit:

Welcome, Welcome, Welcome

I let go of my desire for security

I let go of my desire for affection

I let go of my desire to change the present situation.

A very wise person once said:

EXTENDING THE FRUITS OF CENTERING PRAYER INTO DAILY LIFE & THE FUTURE

The **welcoming prayer** is not simply about healing, but about being created anew. It is Christ casting light upon our darkness, so that we can eventually be transformed into other Christ's.

The best way to understand this practice is to do it.

We will understand it only when we do it, because it is absolutely illogical and irrational.

Close with a 20 min Centering Prayer session and Group Lectio Divina

Assignment- Do Activities for Chapter 10

Read Chapter 11 for next class

Daily Follow Up Activities

Chapter 10

Day 1-- List time and location of your centering prayer practice(s) today

      Centering Prayer session # 1_____

      Centering Prayer session # 2_____

*List the scripture used for your personal Lectio Divina practice_____

 *Practice the Welcoming Prayer

Comment on your reaction to doing this prayer

Day 2-- List time and location of your centering prayer practice(s) today

      Centering Prayer session # 1_____

      Centering Prayer session # 2_____

*List the scripture used for your personal Lectio Divina practice_____

*Practice the Welcoming Prayer

Day 3-- List time and location of your centering prayer practice(s) today

      Centering Prayer session # 1_____

      Centering Prayer session # 2_____

*List the scripture used for your personal Lectio Divina practice_____

*Practice the Welcoming Prayer

Day 4-- List time and location of your centering prayer practice(s) today

      Centering Prayer session # 1_____

      Centering Prayer session # 2_____

*List the scripture used for your personal Lectio Divina practice_____

 *Practice the Welcoming Prayer

EXTENDING THE FRUITS OF CENTERING PRAYER
INTO DAILY LIFE & THE FUTURE

Day 5--   List time and location of your centering prayer practice(s) today

    Centering Prayer session # 1_____

    Centering Prayer session # 2_____

*List the scripture used for your personal Lectio Divina practice_____

*Practice the Welcoming Prayer

CHAPTER 11

EXTENDING THE FRUITS OF CENTERING PRAYER INTO DAILY LIFE & THE FUTURE

The Prayer of Forgiveness

We come now to a practice that may not be easy to do, yet it is at the heart of Jesus' teaching.

We all have people in our lives we need to forgive. This prayer helps us to do just that.

Sometimes we may feel that we don't want to forgive; other times we may feel that we may wish to forgive but we can't. Forgiving is one of the most difficult things to do, yet it is at the core of our spirituality. Try the prayer anyway even if the words, "I forgive you," stick in your throat and you want to scream. See what happens. Do the prayer every day for seven days. You may not feel at the end of seven days that you've forgiven the person, but you'll notice that something has shifted inside you, even if ever so slightly. It's always the <u>intention</u> to forgive that's important, not what we feel inside. Our feelings change from one minute to the next, most of the time without our control so try to ignore them.

This is a powerful prayer. It is another expression of relationship developing overtime and led by the Spirit. You may feel as if you're doing nothing and imagining everything. You don't know if you've affected the person you're trying to forgive. If we believe that we're all connected through the Spirit then trust that you have affected that person even if that person is dead. This is a mystery known only to God. Something does happen. Whatever this "something" is, it's been acknowledged by people who have repeatedly used the prayer.

Forgiveness is at the heart of Jesus' teaching, together with love. The intent you have is as important here as it is in Centering Prayer. Again, you don't need to feel warm toward this person; but if you have the **intention to forgive,** this is all you need. Jesus knows how difficult this can be.

And, if there are people you hate and couldn't possibly forgive, simply ask Jesus to help you. He will. All you need do is wait.

The Forgiveness prayer is a meditation. Although you use your imagination and come up with your own images like seeing the person you wish to forgive and so on, it is still a prayer. Don't let the fact that's it's, at first at least, a guided meditation fool you. The meditation is the prayer.

If you feel more comfortable using your own words instead of a guided meditation, you may choose to do so. What matters is that you do it.

Forgiveness is not easy. It can be all mixed up with hate, revenge, and terrible hurt. It is probably the most difficult thing in the world to do. This is when we have to look at Jesus. Look at his life. He healed, taught, loved, showed compassion and concern to everyone. But they crucified him. Unlike us he was innocent, as a lamb led to the slaughter. He couldn't understand how only a few days before he was hailed by the very people who were now demanding his blood. And yet despite it all what did he do as he hung on the cross? He forgave. He forgave them and by extension forgives all of us time and time again.

The best we can do is to follow him knowing in our hearts that no matter

how many times we fail or mess up he is ready and fully willing to forgive us. So, if this can happen with him and through him and in him, we can hope to do the same.

Sometimes we only think we can't.

We have to try and rid ourselves of any anxiety we may have over this prayer. Remember we're free to choose and whatever we choose is fine with him because our choice is never a one time deal but rather one that we'll probably have to face choosing over and over again.

Prayer of Forgiveness Meditation

By Mary Mrozowski-

Adapted by Gail Fitzpatric-Hopler

Begin with a period of Centering Prayer
Following this, spend a few moments in silence.
Close your eyes, and gently ground yourself I your body;
Scan your body with your inner eye and
Relax each part of your body.
Rest in the area of our chest near your heart.
Breathe.

Focus on your heart and allow our heart to open.
Breath the light of the Spirit into your heart.

PATHWAY TO FREEDOM

Open
Continue to relax your body…

Gently allow the Spirit to lead you through a passageway
That is filled with light, warmth and a welcoming presence.
Invite the Holy Spirit to bring forth a person, living or dead,
Whom you need to forgive.

Or, invite the Holy Spirit to support you as you call to mind
A person that you wish to forgive.

Remain open to whomever appears in your sacred space.
Greet the person by name.

Share your experience of being in relationship with this
Person. Share how you have been hurt,
offended, traumatized. Be specific.

Allow yourself to share our pain with this person.
Relax in the process and remain open.

When you feel ready, tell the person that you forgive them.
Gently say "I forgive you. I forgive you. I forgive you."
Repeat as many times as needed until you feel
Ready to continue the process.

Now ask the person how you have offended,
Traumatized or hurt them.
Wait and listen.

Remain open to the process.

When you feel ready, gently say,
"Forgive me. Forgive me. Forgive me."
Repeat as many times as needed until
you feel compete in the process for now.

Observe your thoughts, feelings and emotions.
Just be present with them.

Allow the person to leave your sacred, safe place.
Invite the person to return at a later time if needed.
Rest in the Sprit.
Take as much time in silence as you wish.

Prepare to leave your sacred place.
Move our of the sacred place…through the door into

EXTENDING THE FRUITS OF CENTERING PRAYER INTO DAILY LIFE & THE FUTURE

The passageway…grounded in your body.
Gently open your eyes when you feel ready.

Close with prayer.

(taken from **The Contemplative Life Program**- "Forgiveness." 2005 pp.13-15)

Long-Range Follow Up Activities

Pick someone you dislike. Try, for at least a week, to see the good in her/him.

This can be hard. You may not want to see the good. Do this anyway and see what happens. Even if at the end of the week you find no good in him, something may have changed in you.

Each day for ten days say something kind about another person or act kindly to him/her. Choose a different person each day.

Go inside yourself. See what you like most about what you see there. Ask Jesus to help you see. Then, try to allow what you like within yourself to grow. Give it warmth, nurture it as you would a baby. Watch it mature. This will take some time, but will be well worth it.

No doubt you feel the beginning of something new in your lives, something that's different for each one of you, something that's precious, and pure, and inviting. Perhaps you're afraid, now that the course is over, that your desire for Centering Prayer will lessen. After all, the support you've had with the classes helped sustain you during this time. Perhaps you may fear that now that you're on your own you may not do the prayers, or you may get bored with them, or feel you cannot find the time, or you may put other things first.

These are all natural reactions.

We all have them. What can we do?

First of all, put the fears aside. Second, turn to Jesus for help. He will see that you do your practices. Third, know that you have begun a journey, a powerful journey inside of you, where worlds will open up, where you'll experience joy and peace you've never known, and in time will be able to extend these gifts to others.

And most important of all: you'll be free, for we are free only when we're free inside ourselves.

Centering Prayer will make this happen.

We have a God who sees only the good in us, and asks only that we accept His love.

He will do the rest.

And, remember, God holds you, and will never let you go.

MEDITATION

Read the following story and comment. Think of where in your life this story relates. Think of how you can live your life seeing others through "Eyes of Christ."

LESSONS ON LIFE

There was a man who had four sons. He wanted his sons to learn not to judge things too quickly. So he sent them each on a quest, in turn, to go and look at a pear tree that was a great distance away.

The first son went in winter, the second in the spring, the third in summer, and the youngest son in the fall.

When they had all gone and come back, he called them together to describe what they had seen/

The first son(winter) said that the tree was ugly, bent, and twisted.

The second son(spring) said no, it was covered with green buds and full of promise.

The third son (summer) disagreed; he said it was laden with blossoms that smelled so sweet and looked so beautiful, it was the most graceful thing he had ever seen.

The last son(fall) disagreed with all of them; he said it was ripe and drooping with fruit, full of life and fulfillment.

The man explained to his sons that they were all right, because they had each seen but only one season in the tree's life.

He told them that you cannot judge a tree, or a person, by only one season, and that the essence of who they are and the pleasure, joy, and love that come from that life can only be measured at the end, when all the seasons are up.⊠If you give up when it's winter, you will miss the promise of your spring, the beauty of your summer, and the fulfillment of your fall.

EXTENDING THE FRUITS OF CENTERING PRAYER INTO DAILY LIFE & THE FUTURE

Moral:

Don't let the pain of one season destroy the joy of all the rest.

Don't judge life by one difficult season.

Persevere through the difficult patches and better times are sure to come some time or later.

Happiness keeps you sweet,

Trials keep you strong,

Sorrows keep you human,

Failures keep you humble,

But only God keeps you going.

<u>Comment by inmate:</u>

As a prisoner we tend to believe that society will always look at us through the eyes of winter. It takes a special person to see the potential fruit in us. That unique person can inspire us to look beyond our own winters and of those around us. I pray that those around me look at me or us, through the eyes of Christ.

CHAPTER 12

SUMMARY

The Active Prayer, The Welcoming Prayer, & The Prayer of Forgiveness will give you freedom.

These prayers will give you a freedom you've never known before, because this freedom is one that lives inside you.

So many people in the world **seem** to be free. They have money, possessions, prestige, power, but inside themselves they're not free. They're imprisoned by their thoughts, emotions, and by themselves. They have yet to learn that they have little, if any, control over their lives; that all they depend on is flimsy and can change at any moment. They fear illness, old age, and death. They have yet to learn that God, the dependable one, is the answer.

This, and only this, makes us free. What goes on around us can be viewed as a bad movie when we have this freedom. Ultimately, this is the only way to live.

Now What?

Let's refresh our memory:

The practice of Centering Prayer opens us to consent to God's loving presence and action within us. This prayer allows us to go deeper and deeper into the ultimate Mystery, God Himself. It purifies us in ways no therapy can; certainly in ways we couldn't do for ourselves. We understand that only God can do this for us. Eventually we begin to recognize and believe in our own goodness. Over time we become aware of the good in others and the connection we have with all people, indeed with the entire human race.

Lectio Divina feeds us in a way nothing else can. Through the Scriptures we learn more about the life of Jesus and we begin to see connections between his life and ours. We're drawn to particular words that can reveal to us unknown factors in our lives that we didn't know. We are able to "see" and understand what is hidden between the lines of Scripture for when we do Lectio Divina the Spirit is very much with us and shows us these things.

The Active Prayer helps to create a clearing in the forest of ceaseless chatter in our minds. We're always filled with thoughts about the past or the future – they seem to be never-ending. When we say the Active prayer, this prayer brings us back to the present moment where God is to be found. All the disruptions, anxieties, fears that thoughts can bring disappear and are replaced by what is real, that is, what is pure, peaceful, and fulfilling. We may find that at the end of the day our thoughts about the life of God are more numerous than thoughts about other things that have occupied our minds.

The Welcoming Prayer helps us to consent and let go of the negative "stuff" in the midst of everyday life. Instead of engaging in troublesome situations that someone has initiated, we turn to the welcoming prayer and welcome the Holy Spirit, while at the same time letting go of the reasons that upset us in the first place. If we can't pray this prayer while the negative situation is happening to us, we're not to get discouraged. We can say it after the situation has passed. The next time will be that much easier to say the prayer while the incident is happening.

The Prayer of Forgiveness helps us to forgive ourselves and forgive others. Perhaps the most difficult of the prayers, it is the key to inner freedom. The most important thing to remember about this prayer is our **intent** to forgive. Our feelings about whether we want to forgive or not aren't important. They change, but our intent doesn't have to.

This prayer may need the special assistance of Jesus because it can be so difficult. Don't be concerned. He's always within you.

For weeks now you've read, listened to your instructor, completed the activities, and, most important, have done all the practices.

No doubt you feel the beginning of something new in your lives, something that's different for each one of you, something that's precious, and pure, and inviting. Perhaps you're afraid, now that the course is over, that your desire for Centering Prayer and the other practices will lessen. After all, the support you've had with the classes helped sustain you during this time. Perhaps you may fear that now that you're on your own you may not do the prayers, or you may get bored with them, or feel you cannot find the time, or you may put other things first.

These are all natural reactions.

We all have them. What can we do?

First of all, put the fears aside. Second, turn to Jesus for help. He will see that you do your practices. Third, know that you have begun a journey, a powerful journey inside of you, where worlds open up, where you'll experience joy and peace you've never known, and in time will be able to extend these gifts to others.

And most important of all: you'll be free, for we are free only when we're free inside ourselves.

Centering Prayer will make this happen. <u>Continue your personal practice</u>, and, if possible, either become part of a Centering Prayer group or form a group on your own.

We have a God who sees only the good in us, and asks only that we accept His love.

He will do the rest.

And, remember, God holds you, and will never let you go.

Bibliography

Arico, Carl A Taste of Silence, Continuum, New York, 1999

Arico, Carl, Fitzpatric-Hopler, Gail, et. Al. The Contemplative Life Program-"Forgiveness" Contemplative Outreach LTD, 2005

Bourgeault, Cynthia Centering Prayer and Inner Awakening, Cowley Publications

Keating, Thomas   Open Mind, Open Heart, Continuum New York, 2001
                       Intimacy With God Crossroad, New York 1994
                       Fruits and Gifts of the Spirit Lantern Books, 2000
                       The Better Part Continuum, New York, 2002

Keating Thomas, Pennington, Basil & Clarke, Thomas Finding Grace in the Center St. Bede Publications, MA 1979

Pennington, Basil Lectio Divina Crossroads, New York, 1998

3480222